Jesus Is Coming

Ingrid Florencia-Kirindongo

TEACH Services, Inc.
P U B L I S H I N G
www.TEACHServices.com • (800) 367-1844

Copyright © 2014 Ingrid Florencia-Kirindongo
Copyright © 2014 TEACH Services, Inc.
ISBN-13: 978-1-4796-0299-5 (Paperback)
ISBN-13: 978-1-4796-0300-8 (ePub)
ISBN-13: 978-1-4796-0301-5 (Mobi)

Published by

TEACH Services, Inc.
P U B L I S H I N G
www.TEACHServices.com • (800) 367-1844

Contents

Introduction

On January 11, 2011, after the massive earthquake in Haiti, my sixteen-year-old son came to me and said, "Jesus is coming soon, and this world is going to end. Look at the earthquake in Haiti! People are dying, and we're not doing anything about it."

He was very upset. I tried to calm him down to the best of my ability. I prayed with him and explained to him and the rest of the family what Jesus said about His second coming and the end of the world. In the books of Isaiah, Deuteronomy, Hebrews, Luke, Matthew, Peter, and others, Jesus gave us clues so that we will know when His coming is at hand. We find examples in Luke 21, Matthew 24, and Isaiah 24 where Jesus delineated the events that will take place before His second coming.

As you look around the world, there are many people just like my son who are concerned about what is happening around them. Most people have a feeling that something is about to happen, but many are not sure what. The economy is struggling and about to collapse, people are losing their jobs and homes, there is political corruption and a love of money, our justice system is corrupt, and people seem to thrive off of more and more debased forms of entertainment. The news is full of stories about incest, pornography, rape, murder, theft, disease, famine, natural disasters, drug abuse, deception, spiritualism, wars, and rumors of wars. In addition to high unemployment rates, gas prices keep rising and home foreclosures are the norm. There is hatred among people groups and false teachers and false Messiahs have arisen and continue to emerge. All of this points to one thing—this world is coming to an end and Jesus is about to come.

Like many people today, according to Mathew 24:3, Jesus' disciples, too, were worried because they went to Him privately and said, "'Tell us, when will these things be? And what will be the sign of Your coming, and of the end of the age?' And Jesus answered and said to them: 'Take heed that no one deceives you. For many will come in My name, saying, "I am the Christ," and will deceive many.'"

Jesus knows that Satan, the prince of this world and the father of lies, operates on the basis of deception. Therefore, He made it clear to His disciples and us as to the signs of His return. These clues keep us focused and help us to be vigilant, awake, and alert as this world comes to an end. May we watch and be ready!

Clue #1

Deception

Jesus said, "'Take heed that you not be deceived. For many will come in My name, saying, "I am He," and "The time has drawn near." Therefore do not go after them'" (Luke 21:8; see also Matt. 24:4).

We read in 1 Timothy 4:1, 2 this exhortation: "Now the Spirit expressly says that in latter times some will depart from the faith, giving heed to deceiving spirits and doctrines of demons, speaking lies in hypocrisy, having their own conscience seared with a hot iron."

And in the final book of the Bible, John warns us about Satan's deceptive work: "So the great dragon was cast out, that serpent of old, called the Devil and Satan, who deceives the whole world; he was cast to the earth, and his angels were cast out with him" (Rev. 12:9).

So how does one avoid being deceived? The Word of God is our only defense against the devil's attacks. When we study the Bible and memorize God's truths, we are equipped to resist Satan and his lies.

As the Bible points out, deception is nothing new for Satan. Revelation 12:7 tells us that in the beginning war broke out in heaven, and Jesus and His angels fought against Satan and his followers. In the end, Satan and one-third of the angels whom Satan had deceived were expelled from heaven. No longer in heaven, Satan set about to deceive Adam and Eve after they were created. His successful plot to mislead Adam and Eve resulted in the couple being sent away from their home in the Garden of Eden (Gen. 3:22, 23).

Throughout history Satan has sought to disillusion people from following God so that they, like him, will lose out on heaven and eternal life. It is his life work to drag as many people down with him as possible. He has studied the weaknesses of humanity and knows what buttons to push. That's why the apostle Paul reminds us that you and I must "put on the whole armor of God, that you may be able to stand against the wiles of the devil. For we do not wrestle against flesh and blood, but against principalities, against powers, against the rulers of the darkness of this age, against spiritual hosts of wickedness in the heavenly places" (Eph. 6:11, 12). Thankfully, God is bigger than Satan and his evil angels and He is ready to protect His children provided they stay connected to Him.

Let's review some of Satan's tactics that he uses to lead people astray:

- He creates doubt; he created doubt in Eve's mind (Gen. 3).
- He distorts the truth; Satan is the father of lies (John 8:44).
- He misinterprets the Bible by mixing truth with his lies (Gen. 3).
- He uses other people such as pastors, friends, government officials, celebrities, or family members to confuse us.
- Through magic and events, he seeks to convince us of his power, such as bringing up the spirit of dead people to converse with those who are living.
- He appeals to our senses:
  - Sight: It looks good (money, fame, riches, etc.).
  - Touch: It feels good (adultery, homosexuality, incest, etc.).
  - Hearing: It sounds good (music, television, etc.)
  - Smell: It smells good (cigar smoke, cocaine, alcohol, coffee, etc.)
  - Taste: It tastes good (unclean food, too much fat, sugary foods, etc.).

Once people fall for these deceptions, they fall into Satan's trap (see Ezek. 28:18, 19).

We must remember that Satan is not our friend. He's a liar and a loser. He lost the war in heaven; he lost the great controversy when Jesus died on the cross; and in the end God will destroy him and all his evil agents forever.

So, my friends, don't be deceived and fall into Satan's trap. Jesus Christ paid the price for you so that you can live with Him for eternity. You just have to trust Him, give your heart and soul to Him, and follow His instructions in the Bible, which someone created an acronym standing for "Basic Instructions Before Leaving Earth."

Another form of deception that Satan uses is by raising up false prophets, false teachers, and false messiahs. Jesus said, " 'For many will come in My name, saying, "I am the Christ," and will deceive many' " (Matt. 24:5). " 'Then if anyone says to you, "Look, here is the Christ!" or "There!" do not believe it. For false christs and false prophets will rise and show great signs and wonders to deceive, if possible, even the elect. See, I have told you beforehand. Therefore if they say to you, "Look, He is in the desert!" do not go out; or "Look, He is in the inner rooms!" do not believe it. For as the lightning comes from the east and flashes to the west, so also will the coming of the Son of Man be' " (Matt. 24:23–27; see also Luke 21:8).

History reveals such false messiahs. In recent decades these individuals have included Jim Jones, David Koresh, Sun Myung Moon, and Jose Louis Jesus De Miranda. These false christs confirm that God's Word is true.

In his last attempt to deceive the whole world, Satan will impersonate Jesus. We can only imagine that Satan will utilize all of the media available today such as the news , the Internet, social media sites, text messages, etc. He will falsely proclaim that Jesus has returned to earth. People will flock to him and welcome him as Jesus, but this is exactly what Jesus warned His followers not to do (Matt. 24:24). Any time you have to go and look for the Jesus that everyone is talking about, the Bible tells us that it is a trick because Jesus indicated that every eye will see Him when He returns (Rev. 1:7).

Not only did Jesus warn His disciples, but Paul warned the church at Corinth that "Satan himself transforms himself into an angel of light" (2 Cor. 11:14). Satan is capable of appearing as if he is an angel of light, but it is all a lie.

Therefore my friends, beware of false prophets, false christs, false teachers, false interpretations of the Bible, false worship services, false books, false pastors, false priests, false science, false doctrines, false messiahs, false popes, false rabbis, false doctors of the Bible, false government officials, false information, false messengers, and false days of worship. All of these counterfeit people, systems, and beliefs have their root in spiritualism and Satan's deception.

To avoid falling into Satan's trap, we must study the Bible for ourselves and ask the Holy Spirit to interpret the Bible for us. We must not rely on anyone but the Holy Spirit to convict and convince us of the truth. And once we determine what truth is, we must follow it, even if we are in the minority. In the end, the false system of worship will enforce Sunday worship. But we must hold fast to God's mandates and keep His ten commandments, including the fourth commandment that marks Saturday as the Sabbath that God instituted at Creation (Deut. 5:6–21; Exod. 20:2–17).

We should never forget what Jesus warned us about the issue of worship in Revelation 12:17: "And the dragon was enraged with the woman, and he went to make war with the rest of her offspring, who keep the commandments of God and have the testimony of Jesus Christ." Everyone who keeps the commandments of God and has the testimonies of Jesus Christ will become the enemy of Satan and of the world. But I would rather be the enemy of Satan than the enemy of God. God is the one we must fear, not Satan or human beings. For in Luke 12:5, we read, "But I will show you whom you should fear: Fear Him who, after He has killed, has power to cast into hell; yes, I say to you, fear Him!"

It is imperative that we study the Bible before it is too late. We must understand its writings if we are to know how to live our lives. For example, Jesus told His disciples to " 'render … to Cesar the things that are Caesar's, and to God the things that are God's' " (Luke 20:25). This verse clearly outlines that we must respect our government as long as it does not infringe, contradict, or go against God's laws. However, when a law of the land supersedes God's laws, we are to follow God! As Christians, our rule of thumb must be "to the law and to the testimony! If they do not speak according to this word, it is because there is no light in them" (Isa. 8:20).

Satan's deceptions and counterfeit will so closely resemble the truth that it will be nearly impossible to distinguish between it except by the assistance of the Holy Spirit and Scripture. That is why it is crucial and eminent for us to eliminate the distractions from our lives and open our Bibles.

Everyone must determine if he or she will obey God or the world. Are you ready to stand firm in defense of God's commandments? Do you have the faith of Jesus? We should not trust our souls to anyone but Jesus Christ. Now is the time to search the Scriptures, fast and pray, and ask God for guidance.

Clue #2

Wars, Famines, and Pestilences

"And you will hear of wars and rumors of wars. See that you are not troubled; for all these things must come to pass, but the end is not yet. For nation will rise against nation, and kingdom against kingdom. And there will be famines, pestilences, and earthquakes in various places" (Matt. 24:6, 7; see also Luke 21:10, 11; Rev. 6:12).

History again proves that God's Word is true. Just in the last 100 years the world has witnessed such wars as World War I, World War II, the Vietnam War, the Iraq War, and the War in Afghanistan. In addition to full-fledged wars, there is constant conflict in the Middle East, and weapons of mass destruction amassed by certain countries threaten to push the world into another world war.

Those of us who lived through the terrorist attacks of September 11, 2011, saw firsthand the destruction that can occur because of hatred. But guess what? These are the beginnings of the birth pains of this earth as time draws to a close.

The twentieth century has proven to be quite deadly, and as we near the second coming of Christ, it will only get worse.

Not only do wars kill people, but diseases and pestilence is becoming more and more common. The news is full of information about viruses and plagues and killer microorganisms. We've seen plagues such as Ebola, SARS, cholera, E. coli, flesh eating bacteria, HIV, AIDS, bird flu, West Nile virus, Salmonella virus, Norovirus, prion diseases, mad cow disease, H1N1, and countless other diseases. In addition to these outbreaks, there are many lifestyle-related diseases that are plaguing the world's population such as cancer, heart disease, and diabetes.

Famines and lack of food also cause suffering to countless men, women, and children around the globe, but especially in Africa, India, Haiti, Thailand, and many other third world countries.

With the Bible as our guide, we don't have to be surprised by wars, famines, and disease. And we do not have to fear these events, for God promises to deliver His people, if not physically, at His second coming when He resurrects the righteous dead who will meet Him in the clouds.

Through my study and reading of the Bible, I've learned that the only way we can prepare for the end and the suffering that may or may not befall us is by studying the Bible, praying to God each day, and depending wholeheartedly on the Lord. We must seek shelter and deliverance in the superior power of our Redeemer, Jesus Christ. Satan cannot take eternal life away from those who are holding securely to the hand of their Savior. Praise God!

Clue #3

Earthquakes/ Powers of Heaven Shaken

"There will be earthquakes in various places … and there will be fearful sights and great signs from heaven" (Luke 21:11; see also Rev. 6:12).

According to the Bible, the powers of the heavens will be shaken (Isa. 24; 34:4; Hag. 2:6, 21; Dan. 7:13, 14). In recent years there have been earthquakes in Portugal, California, Mexico, Haiti, Japan, Virginia, Washington D.C., New York, but these earthquakes, which have brought about massive destruction, are nothing compared to what is coming in the last days as we near Christ's second coming.

Ellen White, speaking about Satan in her book *The Spirit of Prophecy*, volume 4, wrote:

While appearing to the children of men as a great physician who can heal all their maladies, he will bring disease and disaster until populous cities are reduced to ruin and desolation. Even now he is at work. In accidents and calamities by sea and by land, in great conflagrations, in fierce tornadoes and terrific hailstorms, in tempests, floods, cyclones, tidal waves, and earthquakes, in every place and in thousand forms, is Satan exercising his power. He sweeps away the ripening harvest, and famine and distress follow. He imparts to the air a deadly taint, and thousands perish by the pestilence. These visitations are to become more and more frequent and disastrous. Destruction will be upon the inhabitants of the world. The beasts of the field will groan, and the earth will languish. (p. 407)

These things were written more than two hundred years ago, and now we can see them happening. Satan uses the weather to bring destruction and devastation to this earth. He may also use scientists for his purposes. There are those who question whether the government is affecting the weather with such programs at High Frequency Active Auroral Research Program (HAARP). There are other conspiracy theorists who believe that the government is spreading chemicals in the contrail of jets and airplanes, which has earned the name "chemtrail." A quick Internet search brings up information about these two conspiracy theories. Whether these stories are real or not, Satan is capable of using human beings to do his bidding.

After Satan terrorizes the inhabitants of earth through natural disasters, he will persuade people to believe that these things are happening because of the Christians who are keeping God's holy Sabbath day instead of Sunday. He will stir up hatred toward God's people, and many will be imprisoned or killed for taking a stand for their faith.

As we near the end, Satan will increase his destructive powers by sending tsunamis, tornadoes, hurricanes, earthquakes, and all forms of natural disasters on this earth. According to the Bible, all these things must happen before Jesus' second coming and the end of the world. Again, all these things prove that God's Word, the Bible, is true.

In additional to natural disasters, Satan will put signs in the heavens in an attempt to cause fear and divert people's attention away from God. UFOs and talk of aliens and space creatures attract the attention of people around the world, arousing interest in spiritualism and the supernatural world.

Throughout Scripture Jesus, Peter, John, Paul, and other authors tell us to WATCH! Watch the events that happen on a daily basis and compare them with the Bible. It will confirm that we are living in the last days of this earth's history. Now is the time to watch, pray, and ask the Holy Spirit to illuminate our mind and give us oil in our lamps so that we can be ready when Jesus comes. Let's learn from the parables of the ten virgins and make sure we are the wise virgins, and not the foolish ones (Matt. 25:1–12).

In Luke 12:37 Jesus said, "Blessed are those servants whom the master, when he comes, will find watching. Assuredly, I say to you that he will gird himself and have them sit down to eat, and will come and serve them."

Jesus also made the following statement about being ready: "Watch therefore, for you know neither the day nor the hour in which the Son of Man is coming" (Matt. 25:13).

So let us WATCH!

Clue #4

Christians Will be Persecuted

Jesus said, "And you will be hated by all for My name's sake" (Luke 21:17; see also Matt. 10:22; Mark 13:13). Even today Christians all over the world are hated and persecuted for their belief system, and it will only grow worse.

In the face of persecution, we need to remember Jesus' words. Satan hated Jesus way before we were born. If we follow God, Satan places a target on our back because of our affiliation with the King of kings. But Jesus promised us that He would be with us even to the end of the world (Matt. 28:20). We must hold onto that promise when we are faced with tough times.

Jesus warns that those who follow His commandments may be jailed, tortured, and killed. Satan's followers will lay their hands on the saints and will persecute them, deliver them to the authorities, and imprison them. Christ's followers will be brought before kings and rulers and judges for Jesus' sake.

The apostles and Christians throughout the ages and around the world have experienced persecution at the hands of others (Luke 21:12; Rev. 2:10; Acts 4:3; 5:18; 12:4; 16:24; 25:23; 1 Peter 2:13). The day is approaching when Christians will be persecuted again for their allegiance to Jesus and for keeping the fourth commandment that says, "Remember the Sabbath day, to keep it holy. Six days you shall labor and do all your work, but the seventh day is the Sabbath of the Lord your God" (Exod. 20:8, 9).

Also, in the last days, people will be trapped into betraying and hating each other. Parents, brothers, sisters, relatives, teachers, pastors, priests, rabbis, neighbors, government officials, kings, queens, and friends will betray one another.

Even now, although maybe not linked to Christianity, parents are giving their children to the authorities. Children are calling authorities on their parents. And friends are betraying each other just to get a promotion or increase their status at school or in the workplace. This type of disloyalty will lead to betrayal over religion when the time comes.

Satan will destroy the peace in this world and create havoc as time runs out. But God will give His children peace that passes all understanding. In the last days, we must claim God's promises that He will be with us as we endure the trials that come our way, even until the end of the world. So, no matter what we go through, Jesus will go through it with us. We need to claim this promise whenever we feel alone.

Read this insight from Ellen White regarding the reaction of the unrighteous toward the catastrophic events that will fall on the earth—they will blame the Sabbathkeepers, those Christians who refuse to follow the mandates of the government to worship on Sunday, for the devastation:

> Destruction will be upon the inhabitants of the world. The beasts of the field will groan, and the earth will languish.
>
> And then the great deceiver will persuade men that those who serve God are causing these evils. The class that have provoked the displeasure of Heaven will charge all their troubles upon the faithful few whom the Lord has sent to them with messages of warning and reproof. It will be declared that the nation is offending God by the violation of the Sunday-Sabbath, that this sin has brought calamities which will not cease until Sunday observance shall be strictly enforced, and that those who present the claims of the fourth commandment, thus destroying reverence for Sunday, are troublers of the nation, preventing its restoration to divine favor and temporal prosperity. Thus the accusation urged of old against the servant of God will be repeated, and upon grounds equally well established. "And it came to pass when Ahab saw Elijah, that Ahab said unto him, Art thou he that troubled Israel? And he answered, I have not troubled Israel, but thou and thy father's house, in that ye have forsaken the commandments of the Lord, and thou hast followed Balaam." [1 Kings 18:17, 18.] As the wrath of the people shall be excited by false charges, they will pursue a course toward God's ambassadors very similar to that which apostate Israel pursued toward Elijah.
>
> The miracle-working power manifested through Spiritualism will exert its influence against those who choose to obey God rather than men. (White, *The Spirit of Prophecy*, vol. 4, pp. 408, 409).

We are reminded once again that we must always obey God rather than the dictates of others. When we stand by God, we will be victorious.

Clue #5

Increase in Spiritualism

Have you noticed that spiritualism is on the rise? There has been an explosion of television programs and Internet resources on the occult. All of a sudden there is a fascination with spiritualism and an acceptance of this practice. Television programs, movies, books, and video games focus on the underworld and such creatures as vampires, witches, and ghosts. Both kids and adults are drawn into the world of *Buffy the Vampire Slayer*, *The Sixth Sense*, *The Vampire Diaries*, *My Haunted House*, *The Matrix*, the Harry Potter series, and Diablo.

Marketed as a form of harmless entertainment, these shows promote the notion that the living can communicate with the dead and can harness the power of the spirit world. This is Satan's way to deceive and desensitize people so that they will accept spirits, the occult, divinations, palm readers, witchcraft, cards, psychics, astrologers, false spiritual guides, hypnosis, meditations, the New Age Movement, and the New World Order.

What people blow off as innocent fun and entertainment fall into the trap that Satan has set. The apostles warned the early Christian church about this trap, for although the early church didn't have the forms of entertainment we have today, Satan was still working to weave spiritualism into the church. Paul reminded Timothy to not give "heed to deceiving spirits and doctrines of demons" (1 Tim. 4:1).

God knew that Satan would attempt to deceive people through the occult, and that's why He instructed the children of Israel about these types of deceptions, urging them, and us, to stay away from the occult. "There shall not be found among you anyone who makes his son or his daughter pass through the fire, or one who practices witchcraft, or a soothsayer, or one who interprets omens, or a sorcerer, or one who conjures spells, or a medium, or a spiritist, or one who calls up the dead. For all who do these things are an abomination to the Lord, and because of these abominations the Lord your God drives them out from before you" (Deut. 18:10–12).

God again warned His people through the prophet Isaiah: "And when they shall say to you, 'Seek those who are mediums and wizards, who whisper and mutter,' should not a people seek their God? Should they seek the dead on behalf of the living? To the law and to the testimony! If they do not speak according to this word, it is because there is no light in them" (Isa. 8:19, 20).

As Christians we must use this as our rule of thumb. If someone does not speak according to God's Word, it is because there is no light in him or her.

After the terrorist attacks on September 11, 2001, Billy Graham presented a sermon in which he called for a "new spirituality." Again, this made me wonder. I asked myself what new spirit he was preaching about, for the Bible tells us that God is the same yesterday, today, and tomorrow (Heb. 13:8; see also Heb. 1:12). There is nothing new with God (Lam. 5:19). So the question is, is Billy Graham preaching the truth or has his philosophies changed over the years? Again, this is why it is important to trust in God instead of humans. Humans will fail you all the time, but God never changes and His ways are sure.

King David reminds us that "it is better to trust in the Lord than to put confidence in man. It is better to trust in the Lord than to put confidence in princes" (Ps. 118:8, 9).

John the Revelator gives us this warning: "For they are spirits of demons, performing signs, which go out to the kings of the earth and of the whole world, to gather them to the battle of that great day of God Almighty" (Rev. 16:14).

I've learned that Satan uses two great errors to keep people in the dark—the immortality of the soul and Sunday sacredness. The immorality of the soul is pure spiritualism at its best. People believe that they can speak to the death, speak to their loved ones who are dead, be visited by their dead relatives, and receive dreams and messages from their dead family members. The spirits that these people are talking to are none other than Satan and his evil angels. Satan and his evil angels impersonate their loved ones, making them believe that they are seeing and talking to their dead family members. According to the Bible, once a person dies, at that very moment, his or her thoughts perish. The dead cannot praise God, and they do not know anything (Ps. 6:5; 115:17; 146:4; Prov. 11:7; Eccles. 9:5). So how can dead family members talk to you if they do not know anything and their thoughts are gone?

Sunday sacredness is another deception. Many Protestant churches and the Christian Coalition of America think they are honoring God by worshipping on Sunday and by making efforts to unite with the Roman Catholic Church, but they are being deceived in honoring the church that has trampled on God's laws and changed them.

According to Ellen White:

> The dignitaries of Church and State will unite to bribe, persuade, or compel all classes to honor the Sunday. The lack of divine authority will be supplied by oppressive enactments. Political corruption is destroying love of justice and regard for truth, and in order

to secure public favor, legislators will yield to the popular demand for a law enforcing Sunday observance. Liberty of conscience, which has cost this nation so great a sacrifice, will no longer be respected. In the soon-coming conflict we shall see exemplified the prophet's words: "And the dragon was wroth with the woman, and went to make war with the remnant of her seed, which keep the commandments of God, and have the testimony of Jesus Christ." Revelation 12:17. (*The Spirit of Prophecy*, vol. 4, p. 410)

Through spiritualism Satan appears to be a friend of humanity by healing their diseases, showering them with wealth, fame, and honor, and professing to bring a new and more exalted system of religious faith, but it's all a lie. His plan is to deceive people and destroy them in the end. He hates Jesus and His followers and delights in seeing their destruction.

All of the evils in this world will cause the love of many to grow cold: "Because lawlessness will abound, the love of many will grow cold" (Matt. 24:12).

Many people, if they do not stay connected with Jesus, will lose sight of God's promises and will be sucked into a world full of spiritualism. We must remain alert and vigilant if we are to avoid Satan's traps. The devil is a liar. Stay close to God and His Son Jesus Christ, and you will be granted eternal life.

Clue #6

Abomination of Desolation and Christian Flight

" 'Therefore when you see the "abomination of desolation," spoken of by Daniel the prophet, standing in the holy place' (whoever reads, let him understand), 'then let those who are in Judea flee to the mountains' " (Matt. 24:15, 16).

I wanted to know more about this verse regarding the "abomination of desolation" so I examined the books of Daniel, Jeremiah, Chronicles, and Revelation. From these books I learned that the abomination of desolation will happen three times in this world's history and all three times it will be because of the same sins. So the question is, what were these abominations (sins) that caused desolation? Let's hear what Jeremiah said about it.

In Jeremiah 17 God told him to stand in the gate of the people and prophesy. Under a divine mandate, Jeremiah told the people that if they would honor God's seventh-day Sabbath their city would remain forever and that this faithful obedience would lead them into such a relationship with Him that they would be used to convert the surrounding heathen nations (Jer. 17:19–26). However, on the other hand, if they disregarded the holy Sabbath day God warned them that He would allow their city to be burned and become desolate: " 'But if you will not heed Me to hallow the Sabbath day, such as not carrying a burden when entering the gates of Jerusalem on the Sabbath day, then I will kindle a fire in its gates, and it shall devour the palaces of Jerusalem, and it shall not be quenched" (Jer. 17:27).

Unfortunately, the Jews chose to continue worshiping idols and breaking and trampling God's holy

Sabbath day. Thus, they brought upon themselves desolation as prophesied by Jeremiah and as recorded in 2 Chronicles 36:21: "To fulfill the word of the Lord by the mouth of Jeremiah, until the land had enjoyed her Sabbaths. As long as she lay desolate she kept Sabbath, to fulfill seventy years."

In His mercy God showed Ezekiel the abominations that God's people were practicing in the holy place (Ezek. 8). Here the prophet was brought by vision to the door of the inner gate. God showed him the progressively greater outrages His people were committing. In verses 5 and 6 He speaks of an image that provoked Him to jealousy. God proceeded to show Ezekiel the abominations of unclean beasts that had been brought into the house of God, women weeping for Tammuz, and men standing in the temple "with their backs toward the temple of the Lord and their faces toward the east, and they were worshiping the sun toward the east" (Ezek. 8:16).

God specifically instructed the Jews to erect the temple in a manner that would discourage the imitation of their heathen neighbors who worshiped the sun. The ark of the covenant, the focal point of worship, was placed at the western end of the tabernacle. Thus, the children of Israel would face the west, their backs to the rising sun, when they worshiped the true God. Yet, they chose to follow pagan practices to the point that Judah's leading men were actually turning their backs on the temple of God. This was blatant abomination. Ezekiel, Jeremiah, and Daniel all recognized the sins that God's people committed that brought upon them desolation.

All three of them list the pagan practices that were incorporated into the worship of God. Whether it was breaking the second commandment by idol worship; adoring unclean beasts; worshiping Tammuz, a false god of the pagans, or the sun; or breaking God's holy Sabbath day, these practices were classed by God as abominations. In his prayers Daniel pleads with God to forgive the sins the people committed that caused their desolation (Dan. 9:16–18).

So, the first abomination of desolation happened in Daniel's day, which involved the destruction of the temple that was built by King Solomon. The Jewish people trampled on God's holy Sabbath and the Ten Commandments, causing them to go though this time of trouble and desolation.

After God's children were released from Babylonian captivity and the temple was rebuilt, the Jewish leaders erected a mountain of rules and regulations designed to protect them from repeating the sins that had led to their bondage. This was their biggest mistake. Instead of asking God for guidance, they took it upon themselves to correct the problem, which ended up being a bigger problem and burden for the people. As a result, they initiated or added to their traditions instead of following the Ten Commandments that God had given them at Mt. Sinai.

The fourth commandment received the most amendments. As a result of this, more than 500 rules concerning Sabbathkeeping eventually resulted. Some were as ridiculous as you could not spit on the Sabbath because it created mud, which was working on the Sabbath. You could not carry your bag on the Sabbath because it was considered carrying a burden on the Sabbath. You could not leave an egg in the sun on the Sabbath because the sun might cook it. However, by so doing, they created a system of legalism, which gave the false impression that favor with God depended on how well they obeyed the traditions of their elders. However, these same elders created a burden for the people to carry while they themselves did not lift one finger to help. Ultimately the people were led full circle to disobedience again.

I've learned that we cannot change or amend God's laws. We should just obey Him and do His will. The minute we start changing and tampering with God's words we mess things up. And that's exactly what the Jewish leaders did. They messed up God's word, causing the people to obey traditions instead of God's commandments.

Jesus spoke about these hollow traditions when He said, " 'Well did Isaiah prophesy of you hypocrites, as it is written: "This people honors Me with their lips, but their heart is far from Me. And in vain they worship Me, teaching as doctrines the commandments of men." For laying aside the commandment of God, you hold the tradition of men—the washing of pitchers and cups, and many other such things you do.' He said to them, 'All too well you reject the commandment of God, that you may keep your tradition. For Moses said, "Honor your father and your mother"; and, "He who curses father or mother, let him be put to death." But you say, "If a man says to his father or mother, 'Whatever profit you might have received from me is Corban' —" (that is, a gift to God), then you no longer let him do anything for his father or his mother, making the word of God of no effect through your tradition which you have handed down. And many such things you do' " (Mark 7:6–13).

Jesus also expressed His displeasure for their abomination on numerous occasions, especially when He cleansed the temple and expressed His displeasure at the desecration of His holy place (Matt. 21:12, 13).

So, even though their apostasy expressed itself in legalism instead of laxness, it was still based on the same principle upon which all pagan religions are based—that man has god inside of him and that man can save himself by his own works. Jesus, like Jeremiah of old, rebuked this religious system and called it an abomination. " 'You are those who justify yourselves before men, but God knows your hearts. For what is highly esteemed among men is an abomination in the sight of God" (Luke 16:15).

Jesus predicted the second abomination of desolation before His death. As He stood on a hill overlooking Jerusalem, He wept for the city and its inhabitants. He told the disciples that Jerusalem would be destroyed because they rejected Jesus as the Messiah and because tradition was more important than genuine worship. Jesus said, "The kingdom of God will be taken from you and given to a nation bearing the fruits of it" (Matt. 21:43). Israel forfeited their inheritance because of their own sin.

Daniel 8:13; 11:31; and 12:11 speak of the third and final abomination of desolation. These verses predict the formation and ascension of papal power. The time will come when the government will unite with the church to pass a law requiring everyone to worship on Sunday or be killed. It is an indisputable fact of history that the papacy brought into the Christian church the very same practices of paganism for which ancient Jerusalem was destroyed. One only has to do a little research to see how image worship, Tammuz worship, and sun worship were introduced to Christianity during the Dark Ages. Many of these abominations are still with us in the form of statues, candles for the saints, rosary beads, Easter sunrise services, and Sunday worship. Both Catholicism and Protestantism have fostered abominations in God's holy church. The Christian church is mirroring paganism and literal Israel.

Christian churches are repeating many of the same sins of the past and will consequently reap the same punishment of desolation. It is imperative that God's people read the handwriting on the wall and flee from Babylon.

According to Ellen White:

> There is a striking similarity between the church of Rome and the Jewish church at the time of Christ's first advent. While the Jews secretly trampled upon every principle of the law of God, they were outwardly rigorous in the observance of its precepts, loading it down with exactions and traditions that made obedience painful and burdensome. As the Jews professed to revere the law, so do Romanists claim to reverence the cross. They exalt the symbol of Christ's sufferings, while in their lives they deny him whom it represents.
>
> Papists place crosses upon their churches, upon their altars, and upon their garments. Everywhere is seen the insignia of the cross. Everywhere it is outwardly honored and exalted. But the teachings of Christ are buried beneath a mass of senseless traditions, false interpretations, and rigorous exactions. The Saviours' words concerning the bigoted Jews apply with still greater force to the Romish leaders: "They bind heavy burdens and grievous to be borne, and lay them on men's shoulders; but they themselves will not move them with one of their fingers." [Matthew 23:4.]. (*The Spirit of Prophecy*, vol. 4, p. 384)

She goes on to elaborate about the spirit of the papacy:

> The spirit of the papacy,—the spirit of conformity to worldly customs, the veneration for human traditions above the commands of God,—is permeating the Protestant churches, and leading them on to do the same work of Sunday exaltation which the papacy has done before them....
>
> The first public measure enforcing Sunday observance was the law enacted [A. D. 321.] by Constantine, two years before his profession of Christianity. This edict required towns-people to rest on the venerable day of the sun, but permitted countrymen to continue their agricultural pursuits. Though originally a heathen statute, it was enforced by the emperor after his nominal acceptance of the Christian religion.
>
> The royal mandate not proving a sufficient substitute for divine authority, the bishop of Rome soon after conferred upon the Sunday the title of Lord's day. Another bishop, who also sought the favor of princes, and who was the special friend and flatterer of Constantine, advanced the claim that Christ had transferred the Sabbath to Sunday. Not a single testimony of the Scriptures was produced in proof of the new doctrine. The sacred garments in which the spurious Sabbath was arrayed were of man's own manufacture; but

they served to embolden men in trampling upon the law of God. All who desired to be honored by the world accepted the popular festival.

As the papacy became firmly established, the work of Sunday exaltation was continued. (Ibid., pp. 390–392)

At the close of earth's history, we will have to choose which day we will worship God. Will we worship on God's seventh-day Sabbath or on Sunday? The choice is yours. I pray that you will worship God on His holy Sabbath day.

Jesus told His disciples what the last sign of the imminent destruction of Jerusalem that be. He said, "But when you see Jerusalem surrounded by armies, then know that its desolation is near" (Luke 21:20). When the Roman armies surrounded Jerusalem, it was a sign that the city's leaders and inhabitants had passed the boundaries of God's grace and had filled their cup of iniquity. And to the Christians living in the city, this was to be a sign that Jerusalem would soon be destroyed and suffer God's judgment. As soon as the first opportunity arose, these Christians were to "flee to the mountains" (verse 21). All those who heeded the words of Christ were saved from the invading Roman army.

Just as God gave the early Christians a sign of when to flee Jerusalem, so He has given us a sign. He has made it possible for every Christian to know when this world's probationary hour is nearing its close. In Revelation 13 and 14 John provides us with a list of things that will tell us how close we are to the end. But the ultimate sign that will indicate that this nation has filled its cup of iniquity will be when it makes an image to the beast (papacy) by uniting church and state. And this will be done by the passage of a national Sunday law that commands everyone, both great and small, to honor a pagan day of worship. Such an event will be a direct fulfillment of Revelation 13:15–17 and provide assurance that the end of this earth's time is near.

Now is the time to search the Scriptures to determine for oneself God's true Sabbath. According to Exodus 20 and Genesis 2:3, God blessed the seventh day and sanctified it because in it He rested from all His work of creating. Here is the proof we need. The seventh-day Sabbath is God's holy day of rest and worship. Jesus said, "'If you love Me, keep My commandments'" (John 14:15). The duty of all humans is to love God with all their heart and soul.

So the third abomination that causes desolation will happen at the end of this world. The issues that cause the abominations and desolation is the same in all three events. They all have to do with worship and of trampling on God's fourth commandment and His holy Sabbath day.

The time is fast approaching when a national Sunday law will be passed and enforced. When this happens, Christians who keep God's Saturday Sabbath will be persecuted and will go into hiding. Now is the time to *watch* and *pray* and prepare for the final conflict.

During this time of persecution and uncertainty, Jesus has promised to be with us. We must claim His promises that He will help us to persevere until the end.

Clue #7

Man of Sin Revealed, the Antichrist

"Let no one deceive you by any means; for that Day will not come unless the falling away comes first, and the man of sin is revealed, the son of perdition, who opposes and exalts himself above all that is called God or that is worshiped, so that he sits as God in the temple of God, showing himself that he is God" (2 Thess. 2:3, 4).

So who is this man of sin?

> The prophet Daniel declared that the Roman Church, symbolized by the little horn, was to think to change times and laws, [Daniel 7:25.] while Paul styled it the man of sin, [2 Thessalonians 2:3, 4.] who was to exalt himself above God. Only by changing God's law could the papacy exalt itself above God; whoever should understandingly keep the law as thus changed would be giving supreme honor to that power by which the change was made. Such an act of obedience to papal laws would be a mark of allegiance to the pope in the place of God.
>
> The papacy has attempted to change the law of God. The second commandment, forbidding image worship, has been dropped from the law, and the fourth commandment has been so changed as to authorize the observance of the first instead of the seventh day as the Sabbath. (White, *The Spirit of Prophecy*, vol. 4, p. 279)

As we enter the time of trouble and the end of this world, the union of church and state, the increase in spiritualism, and the visible realization of the papal power will be revealed.

According to Bible prophecy, the man of sin is Rome and its papal system (Dan. 7:7, 8). "'Thus he said: "The fourth beast shall be a fourth kingdom on earth, which shall be different from all other kingdoms, and shall devour the whole earth, trample it and break it in pieces. The ten horns are ten kings who shall arise from this kingdom. And another shall rise after them; he shall be different from the first ones, and shall subdue three kings. He shall speak pompous words against the Most High, shall persecute the saints of the Most High, and shall intend to change times and law. Then the saints shall be given into his hand for a time and times and half a time'" (Dan. 7:23–25; see also Dan. 2:40; Rev. 13:1–7; 17:12).

According to history, Babylon was the first beast power, followed by the Medo-Persian, then Greece, and finally Rome, the fourth beast power on earth. The ten horns represent the ten European countries that formed after the breakup of the Roman Empire. History also tells us that three of the European countries were subdued by papal Rome: the Vandals, Ostrogoths, and Heruli.

Please note that it is not my intention to criticize any person or religion. I am simply presenting the facts as outlined in Bible prophecy. When we examine Daniel 7, we find that Daniel mentioning the rise of an institution that will "speak pompous words against the Most High, shall persecute the saints of the Most High, and shall intend to change times and law" (verse 25), which describes the papacy. And, according to Revelation 13, the first and second beast will unite based on common ground and belief system and will thus force the whole world to worship on Sunday. They will call for the legislators to pass laws that specify that if anyone refuses to worship on Sunday according to the law of the land they must be killed.

God has made it clear that the man of sin is the papacy and its mark is Sunday worship. "Then a third angel followed them, saying with a loud voice, 'If anyone worships the beast and his image, and receives his mark on his forehead or on his hand, he himself shall also drink of the wine of the wrath of God, which is poured out full strength into the cup of His indignation. He shall be tormented with fire and brimstone in the presence of the holy angels and in the presence of the Lamb. And the smoke of their torment ascends forever and ever; and they have no rest day or night, who worship the beast and his image, and whosoever receives the mark of his name" (Rev. 14:9–11).

This man of sin is the same institution that thinks to change God's holy seventy-day Sabbath to the first day of the week, Sunday, which we have already learned is an abomination to God: "The earth is also defiled under its inhabitants, because they have transgressed the laws, changed the ordinance, broken the everlasting covenant. Therefore the curse has devoured the earth, and those who dwell in it are desolate. Therefore the inhabitants of the earth are burned, and few men are left" (Isa. 24:5, 6).

Revelation 13 reveals that the first beast is the papacy; therefore, the "mark of the beast" must be some sign of papal authority that stands in direct opposition to the "seal of God." The Roman Catholic Church admittedly changed worship on the seventh-day Sabbath to worship on Sunday. They did this on the basis of their own traditions, stating that the church has authority to act in the place of God. Let's review some of the Catholic writings on this matter:

Question: Which is the Sabbath day?

Answer: Saturday is the Sabbath.

Question: Why do we observe Sunday instead of Saturday?

Answer: We observe Sunday instead of Saturday because the Catholic Church in the Council of Laodicea (A.D. 336) transferred the solemnity from Saturday to Sunday. (Geiermann, *The Convert's Catechism of Catholic Doctrine*, p. 50)

Question: How prove you that the church hath power to command feasts and holy days?

Answer: By the very act of changing the Sabbath into Sunday, which Protestants allow of; and therefore they fondly contradict themselves, by keeping Sunday strictly, and breaking most other feasts commanded by the same church. (Tuberville, *An Abridgement of the Christian Doctrine*, p. 58)

Question: Have you any other way of proving that the church has power to institute festivals of precepts?

Answer: Had she not such power, she could not have done that in which all modern religionists agree with her,—she could not have substituted the observance of Sunday the first day of the week, for the observance of Saturday the seventh day, a change for which there is no Scriptural authority. (Keenan, *A Doctrinal Catechism*, p. 174)

The most authoritative doctrinal council of the Catholic Church was the Council of Trent (1545–1563), which was called to determine "the doctrines of the Church in answer to the heresies of the Protestants" (Kirsch, "Council of Trent," *The Catholic Encyclopedia*). At this critical council, the question of the authority of the church over the authority of the Bible was the subject of long and vigorous debate. The matter was not settled until the last session of the council, and it is significant that the argument that turned the tide in favor of tradition was the change of the Sabbath. This action was cited as the final proof that the authority of the church was superior to the authority of the Bible!

"Finally, at the last opening on the eighteenth of January, 1562, their last scruple was set aside; the archbishop of Reggio made a speech in which he openly declared that tradition stood above Scripture. The authority of the church could therefore not be bound to the authority of the Scriptures, because the church had changed the Sabbath into Sunday, not by the command of Christ, but by its own authority. With this, to be sure, the last illusion was destroyed, and it was declared that tradition does not signify antiquity, but continual inspiration" (Holtsman, *Canon and Tradition*, p. 263).

The well-known Roman Catholic publication *Our Sunday Visitor* published the following quote in the February 5, 1950, edition, chiding the Protestant world for keeping Sunday. It stated: "Practically everything that Protestants regard as essential or important they have received from the Catholic Church. They accepted Sunday rather than Saturday as the day for public worship after the Catholic Church made that change.… But the Protestant mind does not seem to realize that in accepting the

Bible, and observing the Sunday, in keeping Christmas and Easter, they are accepting the authority of the spokesman for the church, the pope."

Protestants likewise recognize that this change rests solely upon the authority of the church. They recognize that there is no divine command for Sunday. "The observance of the Lord's day [Sunday] is founded not on any command of God, but on the authority of the church" (Augsburg Confession of Faith, quoted in *Catholic Sabbath Manual*, part 2, chapter 1, section 10).

"Where are we told in Scripture that we are to keep the first day at all? We are commanded to keep the seventh; but we are nowhere commanded to keep the first day.... The reason why we keep the first day of the week holy instead of the seventh is the same reason that we observe many other things, not because the Bible, but because the church, has enjoined it" (Rev. Isaac Williams, *Plain Sermons on the Catechism*, vol. 1, pp. 334, 336).

In 1859 J. F. Snyder, of Bloomington, Illinois, wrote to Cardinal Gibbons and asked this question: "Does the Roman Catholic Church claim the act of changing the observance of the Sabbath from the seventh to the first day of the week as a mark of her power?"

Through his chancellor, C. F. Thomas, the cardinal gave the following answer: "Of course the Catholic Church claims that the change was her act. It could not have been otherwise, as none in those days would have dreamed of doing anything in matters spiritual and ecclesiastical and religious without her. And the act is a mark of her ecclesiastical power and authority in religious matters."

Does any created human being have the power to change God's law? No! The Bible makes it clear that God's laws are unchangeable and eternal (see Ezek. 20:17, 20; Matt. 5:17, 19). So what does that tell you about Sunday worship? The admission of the Catholic Church proves that the change was based on their own opinion and was not of God. Sunday worship is a man-made day of worship that God warned us to not participate in.

John wrote the following about the beast in Revelation 13:3–8:

> And I saw one of his heads as if it had been mortally wounded, and his deadly wound was healed. And all the world marveled and followed the beast. So they worshiped the dragon who gave authority to the beast; and they worshiped the beast, saying, "Who is like the beast? Who is able to make war with him?"
>
> And he was given a mouth speaking great things and blasphemies, and he was given authority to continue for forty-two months. Then he opened his mouth in blasphemy against God, to blaspheme His name, His tabernacle, and those who dwell in heaven. It was granted to him to make war with the saints and to overcome them. And authority was given him over every tribe, tongue, and nation. All who dwell on the earth will worship him, whose names have not been written in the Book of Life of the Lamb slain from the foundation of the world.

So again this proves that God's Word is true. If we want to have eternal life, we must follow God's mandates and not man-made mandates. The time will come and is soon upon us that the whole world will follow the beast, and those who refuse to follow the beast will be persecuted or killed.

Let's examine what else God is telling us in Revelation 13

> He performs great signs, so that he even makes fire come down from heaven on the earth in the sight of men. And he deceives those who dwell on the earth by those signs which he was granted to do in the sight of the beast, telling those who dwell on the earth to make an image to the beast who was wounded by the sword and lived. He was granted power to give breath to the image of the beast, that the image of the beast should both speak and cause as many as would not worship the image of the beast to be killed. He caused all, both small and great, rich and poor, free and slave, to receive a mark on their right hand or on their foreheads, and that no one may buy or sell except one who has the mark or the name of the beast, or the number of his name. Here is wisdom. Let him who had understanding calculate the number of the beast, for it is the number of a man: His number is 666. (verses 13–18)

Incidentally, one of the pope's titles in Latin is *Vicarius Filii Dei*, which is translated "Vicar of the Son of God." Latin letters have numerical value (e.g. V=5; C=100; D=500, etc.) and the numerical equivalents of the letters in the pope's title total 666. The pope is also called *Dux Cleri*, translated "Captain of the Clergy." This title also totals 666. In Greek, *Italika Ekklesia*, which means Italian church, adds up to 666. The name *He Latine Basieia*, which stands for the Latin Kingdom in Greek, also totals 666. In Hebrew the pope's title of *Romiith* means Roman Kingdom. This name also totals to 666. In Revelation 17:3 it describes the woman (church) as having many blasphemous names. This is another point showing that God's Word is true.

V =	5	*F* =	0	*D* =	500
I =	1	*I* =	1	*E* =	0
C =	100	*L* =	50	*I* =	1
A =	0	*I* =	1		
R =	0	*I* =	1		
I =	1				
U =	5				
S =	0				

112 + 53 + 501 = 666

D =	500	*C* =	100
U =	5	*L* =	50
X =	10	*E* =	0
		R =	0
		I =	1

515 + 151 = 666

According to Ellen White,

> In the book of the Revelation, under the symbols of a great red dragon, a leopard-like beast, and a beast with lamb-like horns, [Revelation 12 and 13.] are brought to view those earthly governments which are especially engaged in trampling upon God's law and persecuting his people. Their war is carried forward to the close of time. The people of God, symbolized by a holy woman and her children, are greatly in the minority. In the last days only a remnant exists. John speaks of them as those that "keep the commandments of God, and have the testimony of Jesus Christ." [Revelation 12:17].
>
> Through the great powers controlled by paganism and the papacy, symbolized by the dragon and the leopard-like beast, Satan for many centuries destroyed God's faithful witnesses. Under the dominion of Rome, they were tortured and slain for more than a thousand years …
>
> Prophecy declares that this power will say "to them that dwell on the earth, that they should make an image to the beast." [Revelation 13:14.] The image is made to the first or leopard-like beast, which is the one brought to view in the third angel's message. By this first beast is represented the Roman Church, an ecclesiastical body clothed with civil power, having authority to punish all dissenters. The image to the beast represents another religious body clothed with similar power. The formation of this image is the work of that beast whose peaceful rise and mild professions render it so striking a symbol of the United States. Here is to be found an image of the papacy. When the churches of our land, uniting upon such points of faith as are held by them in common, shall influence the State to enforce their decrees and sustain their institutions, then will Protestant America have formed an image of the Roman hierarchy. Then the true church will be assailed by persecution, as were God's ancient people. (*The Spirit of Prophecy*, vol. 4, pp. 276, 278)

The third angel of Revelation 14:9 warns all people of the impending conflict when church and state will unite to force worship of the beast and his image. We must tell people about the third angel's message before it's too late, which is the reason of this book.

A lot of information is contained in clue #7, so let's recap what we have discussed in a question-and-answer format.

Whom does the United States command to receive the mark of the beast?

"He [the beast] causes all, both small and great, rich and poor, free and slave, to receive a mark on their right hand or on their foreheads" (Rev. 13:16).

What are those who have the mark allowed to do?

They are allowed to buy and sell (Isa. 24:1–6; Rev. 13:17).

What does Daniel 7:25 declare that the Roman Catholic Church, which is symbolized by the little horn, will do?

"He shall speak pompous words against the Most High, shall persecute the saints of the Most High, and shall intent to change times and laws" (Dan. 7:25; see also Isa 24:5, 6).

"'He shall think to change times and laws.' The change in the fourth commandment exactly fulfills the prophecy. For this change the only authority claimed is that of the church. Here the papal power openly sets itself above God" (White, *The Spirit of Prophecy*, vol. 4, pp. 279, 280).

Speaking to the importance of God's law, Jesus said, "Do not think that I came to destroy the Law or the Prophets. I did not come to destroy but to fulfill…. Whoever therefore breaks one of the least of these commandments, and teaches men so, shall be called least in the kingdom of heaven; but whoever does and teaches them, he shall be called great in the kingdom of heaven" (Matt. 5:17, 19).

According to Paul in 2 Thessalonians 2:3, 4, what did he call the Roman Catholic Church or the little horn?

He called him the man of sin who exalted himself above God. The pope matches this description in title and actions. His title indicates that he is god on earth, and his actions and that of the Roman Catholic Church are of an exalted nature since the church has boldly changed God's laws here on earth.

Satan also exalted himself above God, and we know his fate: "'How you are fallen from heaven, O Lucifer, son of the morning! How you are cut down to the ground, you who weakened the nations! For you have said in your heart: "I will ascend into heaven, I will exalt my throne above the stars of God; I will also sit on the mount of the congregation on the farthest sides of the north; I will ascend above the heights of the clouds, I will be like the Most High." Yet you shall be brought down to Sheol, to the lowest depths of the Pit'" (Isa. 14:12–15; see also Ezek. 28:11–19).

How does one give supreme honor to the Roman Catholic Church, the power that changed God's law?

"Only by changing God's law could the papacy exalt itself above God; whoever should understandingly keep the law as thus changed would be giving supreme honor to that power by which the change was made. Such an act of obedience to papal laws would be a mark of allegiance to the pope in the place of God" (White, *The Spirit of Prophecy*, vol. 4, p. 279).

Which one of God's laws did the Roman Catholic Church attempt to change?

The Roman Catholic Church eliminated the second commandment, which forbids the worship of carved images, they changed the seventh-day Sabbath to the first day of the week, which violates the fourth commandment, and they broke the tenth commandment in two parts to make up for the deletion of the second commandment.

Please note that God's seventh-day Sabbath is for all people, tongues, and nations, not just the Jews. "'Also the sons of the foreigner who join themselves to the LORD, to serve Him, and to love the name of the LORD, to be His servants—everyone who keeps from defiling the Sabbath, and holds fast My covenant—even them I will bring to My holy mountain, and make them joyful in My house of prayer. Their burnt offerings and their sacrifices will be accepted on My altar; for My house shall be called a house of prayer for all nations.' The Lord GOD, who gathers the outcasts of Israel, says, 'Yet I will gather to him others besides those who are gathered to him'" (Isa. 56:6–8).

So, my friends, even if you are not of Jewish heritage, God calls you to worship Him on the seventh-day Sabbath. In His mercy God has opened the door for everyone who wants to follow Him to do so by keeping His laws, the ten commandments that He wrote with His own finger.

1. You shall have no other gods before Me.
2. You shall not make for yourself a carved image—any likeness of anything that is in heaven above, or that is in the earth beneath, or that is in the water under the earth; you shall not bow down to them nor serve them....
3. You shall not take the name of the LORD your God in vain, for the LORD will not hold him guiltless who takes His name in vain.
4. Remember the Sabbath day, to keep it holy. Six days you shall labor and do all your work, but the seventh day is the Sabbath of the LORD your God. In it you shall do no work: you, nor your son, nor your daughter, nor your male servant, nor your female servant, nor your cattle, nor your stranger who is within your gates. For in six days the LORD made the heavens and the earth, the sea, and all that is in them, and rested the seventh day. Therefore the LORD blessed the Sabbath day and hallowed it.
5. Honor your father and your mother, that your days may be long upon the land which the LORD your God is giving you.
6. You shall not murder.
7. You shall not commit adultery.
8. You shall not steal.
9. You shall not bear false witness against your neighbor.
10. You shall not covet your neighbor's house; you shall not covet your neighbor's wife, nor his male servant, nor his female servant, nor his ox, nor his donkey, nor anything that is your neighbor's. (Exod. 20:3–17)

These are God's true commandments that His people will abide by out of love and respect for their Creator. Jesus said, "If you love Me, keep My commandments" (John 14:15).

Where is God's seal found?

The seal of God's law is found in the fourth commandment: "Remember the Sabbath day, to keep it holy" (Exod. 20:8). When the papacy changed the seventh-day Sabbath to Sunday, the seal was taken from the law.

What are God's disciples called to do?

God's followers are called upon to restore God's seal by exalting the seventh-day Sabbath of the fourth commandment to its rightful position as the Creator's memorial and the sign of His authority. Are you willing to uplift God's law and restore His holy Sabbath day to its rightful place? Despite conflicting doctrines and theories that abound, God's law is the one unerring standard to which all opinions, doctrines, and theories are to be tested. As Isaiah said, "To the law and to the testimony! If they do not speak according to this word, it is because there is no light in them" (Isa. 8:20).

God, through the prophet Isaiah, gives this promise: "If you turn away your foot from the Sabbath, from doing your pleasure on My holy day, and call the Sabbath a delight, the holy day of the LORD honorable; and shall honor Him, not doing your own ways, nor finding your own pleasure, nor speaking your own words, then you shall delight yourself in the LORD; and I will cause you to ride on the high hills of the earth, and feed you with the heritage of Jacob your father" (Isa. 58:12–14).

"The time has come for that divine institution [the seventh-day Sabbath] to be restored. The breach is to be repaired, and the foundation of many generations to be raised up" (White, *The Spirit of Prophecy*, vol. 4, p. 285).

Since the time of Adam, God's people have kept the seventh-day Sabbath. Noah, Abraham, Jacob, Jesus, the apostles, and others throughout history have obeyed God's fourth commandment.

Some argue that keeping the seventh-day Sabbath throws them out of harmony with the world, but are we to follow the world or the Creator of the world? Are we willing to follow human traditions instead of the ordained law of God?

Jesus had the following to say about the traditions of men:

> Then the scribes and Pharisees who were from Jerusalem came to Jesus, saying, "Why do Your disciples transgress the tradition of the elders? For they do not wash their hands when they eat bread."
>
> He answered and said to them, "Why do you also transgress the commandment of God because of your tradition? For God commanded, saying, 'Honor your father and your mother'; and, 'He who curses father or mother, let him be put to death.' But you say, 'Whoever says to his father or mother, "Whatever profit you might have received from me is a gift to God"—then he need not honor his father or mother.' Thus you have made the commandment of God of no effect by your tradition. Hypocrites! Well did Isaiah prophesy about you, saying: 'These people draw near to Me with their mouth, and honor Me with their lips, but their heart is far from Me. And in vain they worship Me, teaching as doctrines the commandments of men.'" (Matt. 15:1–9)

Jesus rebukes the scribes and Pharisees because they honored the traditions of the elders instead of obeying God's law. Don't let this happen to you. Remember, Jesus said, "If you love Me, keep My commandments" (John 14:15; see also verses 23, 24). Similarly He also said, "If you keep My commandments, you will abide in My love, just as I have kept My Father's commandments and abide in His love" (John 15:10).

Clue #8

Terrible Time of Trouble and Fearful Sights

Matthew sheds light on the time of trouble in chapter 24, verses 21 and 22: "For then there will be great tribulation, such as has not been since the beginning of the world until this time, no, nor ever shall be. And unless those days were shortened, no flesh would be saved; but for the elect's sake those days will be shortened."

Paul also wrote about perilous times in his letter to Timothy: "But know this, that in the last days perilous times will come: For men will be lovers of themselves, lovers of money, boasters, proud, blasphemers, disobedient to parents, unthankful, unholy, unloving, unforgiving, slanderers, without self-control, brutal, despisers of good" (2 Tim. 3:1–3).

Even now we are seeing some of the things that Paul warned Timothy about. People love money, silver, and gold. There are stories of children killing their parents. Children and adults are unthankful for what they have. People look the other way and engage in unholy acts, abominations, same sex marriages, adultery, fornication, all of which goes against the will of God. Paul also describes the sinful behaviors of men and women in the last days who will not inherit God's kingdom, listing such people as fornicators, adulterers, idolaters, homosexuals, thieves, drunkards, lovers of money, and blasphemers (1 Cor. 6:9–11).

Can you imagine living in this state of sin and decay for a long time? The world in which we are living continues to get worse. If time were not shortened, eventually everyone would die. Thank God for His promise that He will shorten the days for the elect's sake.

The Old Testament prophets spoke about the time of trouble (see Dan. 8:19, 23–25; Isa. 13:9–16; 34:2, 3; 66:16; Jer. 4:8; 6:26; 16:4, 6; 23:19; 25:31–34; 30:23; Micah 6:2; Ps. 79:3). God has warned us through the writings of the Old and New Testaments of the coming conflict. His Word is sure; a time of trouble is coming. Jesus told us in John 13:19, "Now I tell you before it comes, that when it does come to pass, you may believe that I am He." We have already started to see and feel some of this, which is synonymous to the beginning of birth pains. I praise God that He has promised to be with us even to the end of this world provided we keep His commandments and the testimonies of Jesus Christ (Rev. 14:12).

God will not leave His people desolate. He will comfort and protect them through this terrible time of trouble as King David wrote in Psalm 91:9, 10: "Because you have made the LORD, who is my refuge, even the Most High, your dwelling place, no evil shall befall you, nor shall any plague come near your dwelling."

According to Ellen White, God is saying to His faithful few, " 'Stand fast to your allegiance. Help is coming.' Christ, the almighty victor, holds out to his weary soldiers a crown of immortal glory; and his voice comes from the gates ajar: 'Lo, I am with you. Be not afraid. I am acquainted with all your sorrows; I have borne your griefs. You are not warring against untried enemies. I have fought the battle in your behalf, and in my name you are more than conquerors.' The precious Saviour will send help just when we need it" (*The Spirit of Prophecy*, vol. 4, p. 449).

In Revelation 18:2–4 we read God's warning to His people who are still in Babylon to come out of her: " 'Babylon the great is fallen, is fallen, and has become a dwelling place of demons, a prison for every foul spirit, and a cage for every unclean and hated bird! For all the nations have drunk of the wine of the wrath of her fornication, the kings of the earth have committed fornication with her, and the merchants of the earth have become rich through the abundance of her luxury.' And I heard another voice from heaven saying, 'Come out of her, my people, lest you share in her sins, and lest you receive of her plagues.' "

In the last days when God withdraws His spirit from this world, Satan and his evil angels will reign and destroy God's world, for they hate anything that is right and good. But God said, " 'Vengeance is Mine' " (Rom. 12:19). In the end, He will destroy those who destroy His people and His earth (Rev. 11:18).

Now is the time to listen to God's voice and come out of Babylon. Right now, God's angels are restraining the winds of strife; they are holding back the disasters and the time of trouble that must come upon this earth. After everyone has been warned, God will give the command to the angels to loose the winds of strife and disaster, and then the time of trouble will start. At that time, Satan and his evil angels will be allowed to show their true colors without restraint. They will be allowed to carry out their evil plans without reserve. God's people must trust in Him to deliver them from his claws. This time will sift out those who truly believe in God and those who just pretend to do so. True Christians will stand like strong trees that don't break in the fiercest storm. Are you a firmly rooted tree, planted in the Word of God? I pray that all who read this book will trust in God and keep His commandments, including His true Sabbath, so that they will be able to stand like a strong tree in the time of trouble.

Clue #9

Sea and Waves Roaring

In Revelation 12:12 God gives us another warning: "Woe to the inhabitants of the earth and the sea! For the devil has come down to you, having great wrath, because he knows that he has a short time."

It must be painful for God to allow His people to suffer under the wrath of Satan, but in order to prove His innocence before the entire universe, God must allow Satan's true nature to be revealed. But thank God that He has promised to be with us even to the end of the world. We just have to trust Him, call on Him, and claim His promises during our time of distress. Joel 2:32 says: "And it shall come to pass that whoever calls on the name of the LORD shall be saved. For in Mount Zion and in Jerusalem there shall be deliverance, as the LORD has said, among the remnant whom the LORD calls."

One of the clues that will signal the end of history is that the seas will destroy property and claim millions of lives. According to history, from 1993 to 2012 tsunamis hit Japan, Papua New Guinea, El Salvador, Peru, Indonesia, Java Island, Kuril Islands, Russia, the Solomon Islands, Sumatra Island, Chile, New Zealand, the Andaman Islands, Samoa, Haiti, and Thailand.

As we discussed before, according to Ellen White, "In accidents and calamities by sea and by land, in great conflagrations, in fierce tornadoes and terrific hailstorms, in tempests, floods, cyclones, tidal waves, and earthquakes, in every place and in thousand forms, is Satan exercising his power.... Destruction will be upon the inhabitants of the world" (*The Spirit of Prophecy*, vol. 4, p. 407).

After Satan causes all these calamities, he will blame it on God's people. As we have discussed before, Satan will influence lawmakers to develop a law that will force everyone, rich and poor, free and bond, to worship on Sunday or be killed. The same persecution the Christians experienced in the Dark Ages will be repeated again at the end of time. As King Solomon so aptly wrote, "There is nothing new under the sun" (Eccles. 1:9).

Clue #10

Sun, Moon, and Stars

Another sign that the Bible gives us is that "the sun will be darkened" and "the moon will not cause its light to shine" (Isa. 13:10). Joel also contains warnings as to this phenomenon. "The sun shall be turned into darkness, and the moon into blood, before the coming of the great and awesome day of the LORD" (Joel 2:31); "The sun and moon will grow dark, and the stars will diminish their brightness" (Joel 3:15; see also Isa. 51:5, 6).

Ezekiel also prophesied about the heavenly bodies, saying, "When I put out your light, I will cover the heavens, and make its stars dark; I will cover the sun with a cloud, and the moon shall not give her light. All the bright lights of the heavens I will make dark over you, and bring darkness upon your land, says the Lord GOD" (Ezek. 32:7, 8; see also Joel 2:10, 31; 3:4, 15; 4:15).

In addition to the sun no longer shining and the moon turning to blood, the stars will fall. History tells us that the sun was darkened on May 19, 1780, in what is referred to as New England's Dark Day, and when the moon appeared that evening, it was as blood. These events again prove that God's Word is true.

Clue #11

Gospel Preached to the Ends of the Earth

Before Jesus returns to this earth, the gospel will be preached to every tribe and nation. God wants everyone to have a chance to be saved. The people of this world will hear about the good news of salvation and God's love before the close of earth's history so that everyone may decide whom they will follow. God is a God of justice and integrity. He seeks to save all those who will give their hearts to Him.

And yet, following Christ does not mean that the road will be easy. Jesus said that we will be persecuted for His name sake before He comes again: "But before all these things, they will lay their hands on you and persecute you, delivering you up to the synagogues and prisons. You will be brought before kings and rulers for My name's sake. But it will turn out for you as an occasion for testimony. Therefore settle it in your hearts not to meditate beforehand on what you will answer; for I will give you a mouth and wisdom which all your adversaries will not be able to contradict or resist" (Luke 21:12–15; see also Phil. 1:12–14; Acts 6:10).

Now is the time that we must tell people about the good news of salvation. We must share with everyone we come in contact with what God has done for us and what He will do for them too. They need to know about God's true seventh-day Sabbath and the need to keep it holy as God requires.

The fourth commandment, which Rome has endeavored to set aside, is the only precept of the decalogue that points to God as the Creator of the heavens and the earth, and thus distinguishes the true God from all false gods. The Sabbath was instituted to commemorate the work of creation, and thus to direct the minds of men to the true and living God. The fact of his creative power is cited throughout the Scriptures as proof that the God of Israel is superior to heathen deities. Had the Sabbath always been kept, man's thoughts and affections would have been led to his Maker as the object of reverence and worship, and there would never have been an idolater, an atheist, or an infidel. (White, *The Spirit of Prophecy*, vol. 4, p. 281)

As science and technology have increased, the gospel continues to be preached in more and more countries and in more and more languages. Satellite systems take the gospel to countries where missionaries cannot enter. There are also Websites, radio stations, and television stations devoted to taking the gospel to those who haven't heard the message of God's love for humanity. In addition to technology, there are dedicated missionaries, schools, churches, Bible classes and correspondence courses, and audio and video programs that tell others of Christ. Let us continue to share the message with those around us so that they too can have the opportunity to be saved in God's kingdom.

The Conclusion

Jesus' Second Coming

In addition to giving us signs as to events leading up to His coming, Jesus told His disciples about His actual coming. Read what is recorded in Matthew 24: "For as the lightning comes from the east and flashes to the west, so also will the coming of the Son of Man be.… Then the sign of the Son of Man will appear in heaven, and then all the tribes of the earth will mourn, and they will see the Son of Man coming on the clouds of heaven with power and great glory. And He will send His angels with a great sound of a trumpet, and they will gather together His elect from the four winds, from one end of heaven to the other" (verses 27–31).

Many people have different theories of how Jesus will come again, but Jesus made the events of His second coming very clear to His servants so that when it happens they won't be caught off guard.

 When I was a young girl between the age of twelve and fourteen, my older sister Agnes taught us how to give Bible studies and warn people of Jesus' second coming. One day while we were out on the street telling people about Jesus' second coming, an old men who went by the name Chiemie passed by. I approached him and told him that Jesus is coming soon. He yelled at me and said, "You all have been telling people that Jesus is coming for years, but He still has not come." I was so shocked to hear him say that. Even at that young age, it was clear to me that he did not understand nor believe that God, in His love, was delaying His second coming in order to give everyone a chance to hear the message and thus have a chance to be saved.

I praise God that He told us about this delay: "Knowing this first: that scoffers will come in the last days, walking according to their own lusts, and saying, 'Where is the promise of His coming? For since the fathers fell asleep, all things continue as they were from the beginning of creation" (2 Peter 3:3, 4).

Ellen White wrote the following in relation to the seeming delay in Christ's return: "The long night of gloom is trying; but the morning is deferred in mercy, because if the Master should come, so many would be found unready. God's unwillingness to have His people perish has been the reason for so long delay....

"The scoffers mock the waiting, watching ones, and inquire: 'Where is the promise of His coming? You have been disappointed.'" (*Testimonies for the Church*, vol. 2, p. 195).

I do not believe in setting a date for Jesus' second coming. I believe date setting is a tool that Satan uses to make a fool out of people and create doubt. Jesus was clear that no one knows the day or hour of His return, only God knows that (Matt. 24:36).

In His love and mercy, Jesus has delayed His coming so that sinners may have an opportunity to hear the warning and find shelter in Him before the wrath of God is poured out on this sinful world.

Jesus told His disciples that "all things that are written by the prophets concerning the Son of Man will be accomplished" (Luke 18:31; see also Luke 24:44–48; Matt. 16:21; 17:22; Acts 3:13).

In an effort to save everyone who accepts Jesus as their personal Savior, God has given us many warnings and illustrations to help us understand His message. While on this earth, Jesus spoke in parables to the people and told them many things in an effort to help them understand the need for repentance and preparation for the kingdom of heaven.

Following are some of the truths He shared with His disciples:

- "But as the days of Noah were, so also will the coming of the Son of Man be. For as in the days before the flood, they were eating and drinking, marrying and giving in marriage, until the day that Noah entered the ark, and did not know until the flood came and took them all away, so also will the coming of the Son of Man be. Then two men will be in the field: one will be taken and the other left. Two women will be grinding at the mill: one will be taken and the other left" (Matt. 24:37–41).

   These verses tell us that the state of the world at the time of Jesus' return will be similar to the behavior of those living during Noah's time. The Bible tells us that evil thoughts and wicked acts were the norm for the inhabitants of the earth. They disregarded anything spiritual and lived solely for themselves. They degraded the marriage covenant and engaged in violence toward one another. We see this same type of behavior today. The Bible is clear that there will be two classes of people at the end of time. One group will be ready and waiting for the Lord to come. The other group will be absorbed with self and will not be ready when Jesus comes.

- "Watch therefore, for you do not know what hour your Lord is coming. But know this, that if the master of the house had known what hour the thief would come, he would have watched and not allowed his house to be broken into. Therefore you also be ready, for the Son of Man is coming at an hour you do not expect" (Matt. 24:42–44).

- "Who then is a faithful and wise servant, whom his master made ruler over his household, to give them food in due season? Blessed is that servant whom his master, when he comes, will find so doing" (Matt. 24:45, 46).

- "Then the kingdom of heaven shall be likened to ten virgins who took their lamps and went out to meet the bridegroom. Now five of them were wise, and five were foolish. Those who were foolish took their lamps and took no oil with them, but the wise took oil in their vessels with their lamps" (Matt. 25:1–4).

  The bridegroom, Jesus, will come when we least expect; therefore, we must have oil, which represents the Holy Spirit, in our lamp (life) to be able to go out and meet the bridegroom.

- "For the kingdom of heaven is like a man traveling to a far country, who called his own servants and delivered his goods to them. And to one he gave five talents, to another two, and to another one, to each according to his own ability" (Matt. 25:14, 15).

  Jesus has given everyone talents according to his or her abilities. He is coming back when you least expect it, so make sure you are using your talents and sharing with others so that your talents can be multiplied (Matt. 24:16–30).

- "Then He began to tell the people this parable: 'A certain man planted a vineyard, leased it to vinedressers, and went into a far country for a long time'" (Luke 20:9).

  God has entrusted us with this world, and He wants us to bear fruit where He has planted us so that when He returns He can bring in the harvest of the souls we have touched.

- "Then He looked at them and said, 'What then is this that is written: "The stone which the builders rejected has become the chief cornerstone"'" (Luke 20:17).

  The same Jesus that the Jewish leaders and others rejected is the Chief Cornerstone by which everyone will be saved.

- Luke 15 contains the accounts of the lost sheep, lost coin, and the prodigal son. All three parables demonstrate that heaven rejoices when the lost come to Jesus and are saved.

- Matthew 25:31–46 outlines our role as Jesus' ambassadors on this earth. In His name we are to feed the hungry, give water to the thirty, be hospitable to strangers, clothe the naked, and visit the sick and those in prison. When we take care of others, we are really taking care of Jesus.

God would love to shed His light on everyone so that all may be saved, but He does not force anyone to love Him and accept His free gift of salvation. The choice is yours. Whom will you give your heart to, God or Satan? Whom will you worship, God or Satan? I pray that you will choose God and live.

If you choose God, some may try and trick you into believing that Jesus will return in secret or that He will take a few people to heaven at a time. But the Bible makes it clear how Jesus will return. The following verses document the nature of His second coming:

- "For as the lightning comes from the east and flashes to the west, so also will the coming of the Son of Man be…. Then the sign of the Son of Man will appear in heaven, and then all the tribes of the earth will mourn, and they will see the Son of Man coming on the clouds of heaven with power and great glory" (Matt. 24:27, 30). These verses indicate that Jesus' second coming will be bright and visible.

- "Behold, He is coming with clouds, and every eye will see Him, even they who pierced Him. And all the tribes of the earth will mourn because of Him" (Rev. 1:7).
- "Then I looked, and behold, a white cloud, and on the cloud sat One like the Son of Man, having on His head a golden crown, and in His hand a sharp sickle" (Rev. 14:14).
- "For the Lord Himself will descend from heaven with a shout, with the voice of an archangel, and with the trumpet of God. And the dead in Christ will rise first. Then we who are alive and remain shall be caught up together with them in the clouds to meet the Lord in the air. And thus we shall always be with the Lord" (1 Thess. 4:15–18).

No one knows the day and hour of Jesus' second coming. That is why Jesus told us to watch and pray. Just as in the days of Noah, Jesus will return when people least expect it. As in Noah's day, moral decay was rampant. They were eating and drinking until the rain began to fall and the water began to rise. They were not prepared. It will be the same when Jesus comes again.

As we witness the degradation of the world around us, we know that our redemption draws near. "Watch therefore, and pray always that you may be counted worthy to escape all these things that will come to pass, and to stand before the Son of Man" (Luke 21:36).

Now is the time that we should watch and pray because we do not know when Jesus will return. In the Gospel of Mark we find these words: "Take heed, watch and pray; for you do not know when the time is…. Watch therefore, for you do not know when the master of the house is coming—in the evening, at midnight, at the crowing of the rooster, or in the morning—lest, coming suddenly, he find you sleeping" (Mark 13:33–36). John the Revelator likens Christ's coming to that of a thief: "Therefore if you will not watch, I will come upon you as a thief, and you will not know what hour I will come upon you" (Rev. 3:3).

We are living in the last days of this earth's history. Now is the time to clean up our life and put our house in order so that when our case comes up for review before God we will be covered by the blood of Jesus. In Proverb 28:13 we learn that "He who covers his sins will not prosper, but whoever confesses and forsakes them will have mercy."

According to Ellen White, "All who would have their names retained in the book of life, should now, in the few remaining days of their probation, afflict their souls before God by sorrow for sin, and true repentance. There must be deep, faithful searching of heart. The light, frivolous spirit indulged by the majority of professed Christians must be put away. There is earnest warfare before all who would subdue the evil tendencies that strive for the mastery" (*The Spirit of Prophecy*, vol. 4, p. 314).

Will you be ready? Among Christians and non-Christians, people are worried. They see the corruption of government and the increase of natural disasters; they see the evilness of humanity and the disregard that people have for the life of others. As the signs point toward a cataclysmic event, many are preparing to save themselves instead of turning to the only One who can save them. Many people are preparing underground bunkers and stockpiling goods in preparation for world destruction, but their efforts are futile. No government, no police force, no scientists, no guns, and no psychics will save you—only Jesus Christ can save you!

In summary, Jesus' second coming will be:

- A real and physical event (Rev. 16:18)
- A literal event (Acts 1:9–11)
- A visible event (Rev. 1:7)
- A glorious event (Matt. 25:31)
- A worldwide event (Matt. 24:26, 27)
- An audible event (1 Thess. 4:16)
- A bright event (2 Thess. 2:8)
- A decisive event (Matt. 24:29–31)
- Many people will be unprepared just like the days of Noah and Lot. Luke 17:26-30

Sadly, many people will be unprepared just like in the days of Noah and Lot. "And as it was in the days of Noah, so it will be also in the days of the Son of Man: They ate, they drank, they married wives, they were given in marriage, until the day that Noah entered the ark, and the flood came and destroyed them all. Likewise as it was also in the days of Lot: They ate, they drank, they bought, they sold, they planted, and they built; but on the day that Lot went out of Sodom it rained fire and brimstone from heaven and destroyed them all. Even so will it be in the day when the Son of Man is revealed.… Whoever seeks to save his life will lose it, and whoever loses his life will preserve it" (Luke 17:26–33).

We must "watch therefore, and pray always that you may be counted worthy to escape all these things that will come to pass, and to stand before the Son of Man" (Luke 21:36). Jesus has told us the signs of His coming so that we may be ready (John 14:29).

It is imperative to take care that no one deceives you. And the only way to avoid deception is to know what the Bible says. Will you stand firm on the Word of God, or will you fold to the ways of the world? What type of Christian are you? Are you like a switch that turns on and off? Are you like a canoe, needing to paddle? Are you like a turtle, hiding when things get tough? Are you like an ostrich, putting your head in the sand? Are you like a yo-yo, going up and down? Are you like an eagle, soaring high in the sky? Are you like a butterfly, changing from a caterpillar to a beautiful butterfly? Or are you like a lion that is ready to prove it is tough?

No matter what we are going through, we must keep in mind that this world is not our home. God did not make us to live in misery and suffering. One day He will put an end to this world of sorrow and sin. He's ready to save all those who call upon His name and want to follow Him. Now is the time to make your decision. Who will you give your heart to? Who will you worship?

I pray that you will make the right decision and follow Jesus Christ, the Messiah and Savior of this world.

Bibliography

Geiermann, Peter. *The Convert's Catechism of Catholic Doctrine.* London: 1934.

Holtsman, J. H. *Canon and Tradition.* Luduigsburg: Heinrich Julius Holtzman, 1859.

Keenan, Rev. Stephen. *A Doctrinal Catechism.* New York: Edward Dunigan and Brothers, 1851.

Kirsch, J. P. "Council of Trent." *The Catholic Encyclopedia.* New York: Robert Appleton Company, 1912.

Tuberville, Rev. Henry. *An Abridgement of the Christian Doctrine.* New York: Edward Dunigan and Brothers, 1833.

White, Ellen G. *The Spirit of Prophecy.* Vol. 4. 1884.

White, Ellen G. *Testimonies for the Church.* Vol. 2. Mountain View, CA: Pacific Press Publishing Association, 1871.

Williams, Rev. Isaac. *Plain Sermons on the Catechism.* Vol. 1. London: 1882.

We invite you to view the complete
selection of titles we publish at:

www.TEACHServices.com

Please write or email us your praises, reactions, or
thoughts about this or any other book we publish at:

TEACH Services, Inc.
P U B L I S H I N G
www.TEACHServices.com ● (800) 367-1844

P.O. Box 954
Ringgold, GA 30736

info@TEACHServices.com

TEACH Services, Inc., titles may be purchased in bulk for
educational, business, fund-raising, or sales promotional use.
For information, please e-mail:

BulkSales@TEACHServices.com

Finally, if you are interested in seeing
your own book in print, please contact us at

publishing@TEACHServices.com

We would be happy to review your manuscript for free.

www.ingramcontent.com/pod-product-compliance
Lightning Source LLC
Chambersburg PA
CBHW050357100426
42739CB00015BB/3428